VEGAN INSTANT POT COOKBOOK

Logan Baker

CONTENTS

INTRODUCTION

Veganism, as a global phenomenon, became a popular choice for millions of people around the globe. What's driving more and more conscious people to choose a plant-based lifestyle? Health, ethical, altruistic, environmental reasons? In case you were wondering why people worldwide follow a vegan diet, the medical database contains a large amount of information.

On the other hand, an Instant Pot has a permanent space on kitchen counters worldwide. If you go vegan and own an Instant Pot, this recipe collection may become your steady kitchen companion. It includes carefully selected vegan recipes, from breakfast to soups and snacks. If you are thinking of going vegan, you will find lots of useful information in these recipes, including tips, serving ideas and nutritional analysis. If you are wondering what a home-cooked meal looks like with animal products out of the table, this recipe collection will give you the best answers. Vegan Instant Pot meals have a power that brings families together. The Instant Pot vegan recipes can help you build good eating habits, as well as stay healthy and fit for life. These recipes offer a health-oriented lifestyle to you; they are super tasty, budget-friendly and very convenient. Nevertheless, veganism is more than a trend!

Benefits of a Vegan Lifestyle

Can you follow a vegan diet and still get all necessary nutrients? Are there the evidence-based benefits of a vegan diet? If you are not a vegan, it is perfectly normal to have doubts about dietary change. In the following lines, we will try to explain the findings from the scientifically credible studies that have proven the benefits of a vegan dietary regimen.

1. Health benefits of a vegan diet.

Following a balanced plant-based diet ensures many health benefits, including the prevention of many chronic diseases. A vegan menu is loaded with whole foods such as fresh fruits, nutrient-dense vegetables, legumes, whole grains, and nuts. The nutrients in those foods are vital for the maintenance of a healthy body. In fact, people who eat mostly plants as part of their daily diet have a reduced risk of many serious diseases. However, you should consume a range of different foods to make sure you get essential vitamins, minerals, and amino acids. In other words, you should provide your body with essential nutrients that must come from food; the human body can not synthesize essential nutrients on its own or it can not make them in sufficient quantity.

As for the carcinogenicity of the consumption of red meat and processed meat, The World Health Organization (WHO) announced, "Meat consists of multiple components, such as harm iron. Meat can also contain chemicals that form during meat processing or cooking. For instance, carcinogenic chemicals that form during meat processing include N-nitrous compounds and polycyclic aromatic hydrocarbons. Cooking of red meat or processed meat also produces heterocyclic aromatic amines as well as other chemicals including polycyclic aromatic hydrocarbons, which are also found in other foods and in air pollution. Some of these chemicals are known or suspected carcinogens, but despite this knowledge it is not yet fully understood how cancer risk is increased by red meat or processed meat." (October 2015)

A plant-based diet can help you prevent many serious diseases. If you consume hyper-processed food, sugar, trans fats, white flour, chemicals, and inflammatory foods, meat, and dairy products, you're more likely to develop chronic diseases. On the other hand, cooking at home can help you adopt healthy eating habits and lose weight in a natural way. A plant-based diet is loaded with fiber, whole grains, and fresh fruits that boost your metabolism and improve digestion, as well as make you feel fuller longer. Further, fresh fruits and vegetables are lower in calories, fats and bad cholesterol than animal products. Take tofu vs. chicken for example. Tofu contains 70 calories, 1 g of saturated fat, and 0 mg of total cholesterol per 100 grams of products. On the other hand, there are 219 calories, 3.5 g of saturated fat, and 78 mg of cholesterol in 100 grams of chicken. Are these reasons good enough for you?

Numerous studies have shown that eating a vegan diet may help prevent prostate cancer, colon cancer, and breast cancer. It can also cure fatigue, arthritis, osteoporosis, reflux, cardiovascular disease, chronic allergies, eczema, psoriasis, macular degeneration, and auto-immune disease. A vegan diet high in fruits and vegetables can help you regulate blood pressure (it can cut systolic blood pressure by more than 10 points).Obviously, our food is the best medicine.

2. A well-planned vegan diet can make you stronger and more energetic.
Besides being super healthy, eating plant-based diet also provides many physical benefits. What's more, a plant-based diet leads to lower Body Mass Index (BMI). A vegan diet may help you lose weight in a natural way. The Adventist Health Study (AHS) has proven that vegans have lower BMI than people who eat animal products such as dairy, eggs, seafood, and especially red meat.

If you tend to gain lean muscle, you should focus on eating foods that can help you build tissues and exercising regularly. Numerous plant-based foods can help you build muscle and get stronger. Vegan muscle-building foods include soybeans, black, kidney and pinto beans, quinoa, brown rice, chickpeas, buckwheat, peanuts, almonds, tofu, protein powders (hemp, soy, and pea). Focus on nutritious, protein-packed foods that can stimulate muscle growth. Put simply, if your goal is to be happy, healthy and strong, use energy from a plant-based food.

3. A well-balanced vegan diet can make you look and feel fantastic.

"You are what you eat", it may sound like a cliché, but it is true! Your diet can significantly affect the health of your skin. Luckily, there are easy solutions to make your skin glow from the inside out. The best way to keep your skin healthy is by ensuring that you're eating a variety of good and nutritious foods. Vitamin C is needed for a healthy, radiant skin. A vegan diet is loaded with foods with high vitamin C content such as citrus fruits, bell peppers, leafy greens, broccoli, strawberries, and kiwi fruit. Walnuts are a great source of omega-3 and omega-6 fatty acids, which make them a great food for healthy skin. Further, nuts and seeds are an excellent source of vitamin E, which is an important antioxidant and anti-aging vitamin. Vitamin A is also a powerful vitamin for younger looking skin. You should eat carrots, apricots, mango, and broccoli. Forget the Botox and eat your way to a healthier and younger skin. Top anti-aging foods include mushrooms, avocado, blueberries, pomegranate, watermelon, tomato, figs, red cabbage, cucumber, sweet potatoes. As for beverages, green tea, red wine, and almond milk can protect your skin from aging. When it comes to the herbs and spices, you should eat parsley, garlic, turmeric, and saffron. These foods are not only great for your skin, but they also help you stay young and healthy. Ultimately, when you look great, you feel great!

4. Showing compassion for animals can improve your well-being.

Pythagoras said. "For as long as men massacre animals, they will kill each other. Indeed, he who sows the seed of murder and pain cannot reap joy and love." There are many stories of animals saving human lives; in fact, compassion is natural and instinctive for all beings. Compassion makes us feel good. There is plenty of evidence that animals have emotions, thoughts, and social connections. If you're a pet owner, you are aware of these facts. Veganism can help you develop an ability to "see the big picture". It can inspire you to give and share with others. Compassion will give you many possibilities, including a higher quality of life. Climate change, animal rights and welfare, health and wellbeing... there are numerous reasons to embrace a plant-based lifestyle, especially in the past few decades.

What do Vegans Eat? Six Essential Nutrients

What a healthy vegan should eat in a day? There are six main groups of key nutrients you should include in your diet.

CARBOHYDRATES are necessary for our body to function properly. Our body turns carbs into glucose, which is a vital source of fuel for the human body. You should consume a variety of simple carbohydrates such as fresh fruits and vegetables, as well as whole grains such as oats, whole-wheat bread, quinoa, barley, and brown rice.

You should eat a variety of carbs on a daily basis to provide your body with energy. However, the type of carbs you eat matters since there are "good" and "bad" carbs. Opt for fiber-rich vegetables, whole grains, and natural sugar sources instead of refined grains and highly processed products. Limit intake of food and drinks that are high in sugar such as ketchup, fruit juice, sports drinks, granola, flavored coffee and tea, pre-made soup, canned vegetables, and so on.

PROTEINS provide the building blocks of our tissues; in fact, every cell contains protein (it consists of smaller units called amino acids). The good news is that you do not need to consume animal products for a good health. Your body can create some amino acids on its own, but it can also create complete proteins from the plant-based foods. Ten to thirty-five percent of your daily calories should come from protein. Adding protein to your plant-based diet is an easy task. Simply throw some beans into your salads or add seeds to your smoothies. Choose healthy snacks such as peanuts, kale chips or homemade protein bars. Focus on a variety of proteins to ensure your body are getting all essential amino acids. The best sources of plant-based protein include:

- Soy products – milk, tofu, and tempeh contain plenty of protein and key nutrients;
- Lentils – red and green lentils are high in protein;
- Peanuts – this is a great source of protein, cheap and available. You can eat peanut butter, homemade peanut cookies, or enjoy roasted peanuts as a snack;

- Quinoa – this is very nutritious food. One cup of cooked quinoa delivers 8 grams of protein;
- Seitan – it is made from wheat gluten, the main protein of wheat. Seitan is a quite versatile food so you can use it to make vegan steaks, stews, moussaka, lasagna and so forth. It offers 21 grams of protein per 1/3 cup;
- Beans with rice – one cup of this classic vegan meal delivers 7 grams of protein;
- Protein-rich vegetables – broccoli, dark-colored leafy greens, and mushrooms are the most important sources;
- Potatoes – there are 8 grams of protein in a large-sized cooked potato;
- Seeds – chia seeds and hemp seeds are extremely important in a vegan diet since they are complete sources of protein;
- Chickpeas – you can add chickpeas and hummus to sandwiches, salads, stews, soups, spreads, and vegan burgers. Two tablespoons of hummus deliver 3 grams of protein.

FAT gives your body energy and supports its proper function. It produces hormones and keeps you warm naturally. It supports vital body's functions such as building cells and muscle movement. In addition, fats can help you absorb vitamins A, K D, and E.

There are "bad" fats and "good" fats. In general, you should avoid bad, saturated fats; although most of them come from animal products, keep in mind that palm oil and cocoa butter contain saturated fats, too. Opt for smart options such as cashews, almonds, walnuts, chia seeds, and cold pressed vegetable oils that contain omega-3-fatty acids. Other healthy choices include avocado, coconut, and most seeds.

VITAMINS can strengthen your immune system and help your body fight diseases; furthermore, they are essential for normal growth and development. There are 13 essential vitamins. Vitamins not only help you live longer by preventing serious diseases, but they also support many physiological functions.

Eating a diversity of colorful fruits and vegetables can be the best way to get a complete range of the vitamins that are beneficial to your body. Each color indicates an abundance of different nutrients. Red fruits and vegetables (for example, tomatoes, red pepper, strawberries, beets, cherries, and cranberries) can protect you from cancer. Green foods (e.g. broccoli, asparagus, leafy greens, green beans, arugula, lettuce, and peas) are essential for blood and bone health. Blue and purple plants (e.g. blueberries, purple cabbage, eggplant, plums, prunes, and purple grapes) fight inflammation and slow aging naturally. Brown fruits and vegetables (e.g. mushrooms, potatoes, and onions) can keep your bones strong and protect against cancer. Orange and yellow fruits and vegetables (e.g. oranges, lemon, banana, carrots, papaya, pineapple, grapefruit, peaches, mango, and squash) can boost your immune system, promote eye health, and increase blood flow. To conclude, eat the rainbow and you will be just fine!

What is the biggest issue in a plant-based diet? As you probably already know, it is vitamin B12. Vegans can develop B12 deficiency, but there are other groups that are at risk. Adults over 50 are at risk too, as well as women who take birth control pills and alcoholics. Then, people with colitis and Crohn's disease are at a higher risk. Many meat eaters are B12 deficient so we can conclude that it is not just a vegan problem. You should consume fortified foods such as nutritional yeast, fortified cereals, and plant-based milk. Another option is to take supplements. Last but not least, you should maintain a healthy gut to improve the absorption of vitamin B12.

MINERALS are essential for many body functions.

There are 16 essential minerals. The five major minerals in the human body are calcium, magnesium, sodium, phosphorus, potassium. Calcium provides healthy bones and proper function of nerves; it also helps muscles contract and protects your immune system. Vegan sources of calcium include fortified soy products, sesame seeds, tahini paste, cocoa powder, legumes, calcium-fortified plant milk, and greens.

Magnesium is needed for more than 300 biochemical reactions in the body. These include proper nerve and muscle function, immune system health, nerve transmission, strong bones and teeth. Magnesium can also regulate blood glucose; it can help improve a woman's health and eliminate premenstrual syndrome. Magnesium-rich foods include leafy greens vegetables, cashews, almonds, artichokes, Brazil nuts, pecans, millet, buckwheat, and molasses.

Your body needs sodium for proper nerve transmission and muscle contraction. You can find sodium in a table salt, soy sauce, bread, and some vegetables. As for phosphorus, it is needed for strong bones, acid-base balance, and tissue repair. In fact, calcium and phosphorus are the most plentiful minerals in the human body. Phosphorus helps to grow and maintain cells, maintain a proper heartbeat, reduce muscle pain, and manage energy levels in your body. Most foods contain phosphorus. Foods that are rich in protein are also excellent sources of phosphorus. These include nuts, seeds, beans, whole grains, potatoes, garlic, dried fruit. In other words, when your diet includes enough protein, you do not need to worry about phosphorus. Potassium can help to maintain good blood pressure, as well as a balance of acids and bases in the human body. In addition, it can help your nerves and kidneys work properly. Vegan sources of potassium include potatoes, tomatoes, avocado, banana, orange juice, dried fruits (prunes, raisins, apricots, and dates), greens, peas, and beans.

WATER is a compound that your body can't make. For an adult human being, up to 60 percent of their body weight comes from water. The human body can't survive more than a couple of days without water. Needless to say, water is involved in every function of our body, from circulation to digestion. Water improves your brain function, concentration, and physical performance; it delivers nutrients to cells, hydrates the body, and prevents constipation. A healthy adult needs at least 2 liters of water per day. When you exercise, it is recommended to have five percent more body water than an average person has. When all is said and done, a well-planned vegan diet and Instant Pot home-cooked meals can fulfill all your nutritional requirements.

How You'll Benefit from the Vegan Instant Pot Recipes

Do you think that sticking to a vegan diet is difficult because you do not have that much time to plan meals, go grocery shopping and cook? Luckily, you can save your valuable time with the help of an Instant Pot. An Instant Pot is a programmable multi-cooker that is designed to use a super-heated steam to cook your food under pressure. With 14 preset buttons, you will be excited about your Instant Pot.

The "Manual" is a basic button since you can adjust the time, temperature and pressure. You can cook most foods with this button. Moreover, you can caramelize onions and sauté vegetables in your Instant Pot without using additional pans. Sautéing is a good technique to enhance flavors and aromas of your food. The "Keep Warm" button is a great feature to keep your food warm until you are ready to eat; it's perfect for when you have friends over. The Instant Pot also works as a warming pot as well as a mini smart oven. The "Slow Cook" function works as any slow cooker you can buy everywhere. Other fancy buttons are designed for the particular type of food as their name indicates. You will see the buttons that say Soup, Meat/Stew, Poultry, Bean/Chili, Rice, Porridge, and Multigrain; they are extremely helpful when you're a newbie so you are not sure how long should you cook a certain type of food.

In practice, you should place the ingredients in the inner pot; then, you should secure the cooker's lid and press the right button; the next step, let your cooker do its job, sit back and relax. Afterwards, once the cooking cycle is complete, you should realize the pressure. The Instant Pot uses the third-generation technology to achieve great results in the kitchen. It uses an innovative formula that supports healthy cooking and environmental sustainability. There's a lot to love about vegan diet and Instant Pot!

The Instant Pot replaces eight different appliances in your kitchen; it can work as a pressure cooker, slow cooker, steamer, sauté pan, rice cooker, warming pot, cooking pot, and yogurt maker. It utilizes an automated cooking process to cook your vegan meals to absolute per-fection. Despite the common belief, the Instant Pot promotes a well-balanced vegan diet, clean eating, and whole foods. In fact, a vegan diet and Instant Pot go hand in hand since you cook many different types of vegan dishes in a short amount of time. Setting an Instant Pot to cook your meal sounds like a good idea, right? Time-saving is one of the greatest ben-efits of the Instant Pot. Vegan meals such as beans, rice, soups, stews, and porridges require little to no preparation while easy press-and-go functions on your Instant Pot can save you tons of time! It's the perfect tool for potlucks, dinner parties, holidays, and kid's birthdays. It's like having an extra burner in the kitchen.

If you tend to simplify things, you should embrace a plant-based diet and practical kitchen tools such as an electric pressure cooker. The Instant Pot is a super-sophisticated machine that promotes minimalism by cooking different types of food in only one pot. If you are batch-cooking, you will be obsessed with your Instant Pot. Did you know that you could bake cakes in the Instant Pot? The Instant Pot vegan meals are easy to make and fun to eat!

Besides being convenient, cooking in a pressure cooker tends to keep valuable micronutri-ents and macronutrients from plants; it is an important part of maintaining a healthy diet. The Instant Pot has an airtight lid that prevents nutrients to escape from the sealed environ-ment; key nutrients are retained rather than boiling away. A well-balanced vegan diet that promotes nutrient-rich food sources and home-cooked meals are vital for growth, good health, and disease prevention.

Since the Instant Pot utilizes hyper-pressurized environment, it is evident that it uses less energy to cook your food; it uses up to 70% less energy than conventional methods. There-fore, it will cut down your electric bill and it is beneficial for the Mother Earth, too.

The Instant Pot is all-in-one multi-cooker; it is perfect for beans chilies, lentil dishes, soups, and stews, but you can cook almost all your meals under pressure. The recipes in this collec-tion are grouped into six main categories: BREAKFAST, SOUPS, MAIN COURSES, SIDE

DISHES, SNACKS, and KETO-FRIENDLY RECIPES. Every recipe includes the ingredient list (for your grocery list), clear and detailed directions, the recommended serving size for a successful portion control, and nutritional analysis so you can easily plan your meals and track your calories. You can also find many useful hints and tips, so this cookbook can eventually make you a real culinary expert. Additionally, in order to make everyone happy, this recipe collection contains 13 vegan, keto-friendly recipes that are low in carbs and high in protein. Let's start our culinary journey!

BREAKFAST

1. Oatmeal with Pumpkin and Cherries

(Ready in about 25 minutes | Servings 4)

INGREDIENTS

2 ½ pounds pumpkin, cleaned and
 seeds removed

1/2 cup rolled oats

1/2 teaspoon ground cinnamon

A pinch of salt

A pinch of grated nutmeg

4 tablespoons dried berries

1 cup water

DIRECTIONS

- Add 1 ½ cups of water and a metal trivet to the Instant Pot. Now, place the pumpkin on the trivet.
- Secure the lid. Choose the "Manual" mode and cook for 12 minutes under High pressure. Once cooking is complete, use a natural release; carefully remove the lid.
- Then, purée the pumpkin in the food processor.
- Wipe down the Instant Pot with a damp cloth. Add the remaining ingredients to the Instant Pot, including the pumpkin purée.
- Secure the lid. Choose the "Manual" mode and cook for 10 minutes under High pressure. Once cooking is complete, use a natural release; carefully remove the lid.

Per serving: 201 Calories; 1.1g Fat; 51.8g Carbs; 5g Protein; 31.9g Sugars

2. Barley Porridge with Butternut Squash

(Ready in about 45 minutes | Servings 4)

INGREDIENTS

2 tablespoons olive oil divided

2 cloves garlic, minced

1/2 cup scallions, chopped

2 cups butternut squash, peeled and
cubed

1/2 teaspoon turmeric powder

2 cups barley, whole

4 ½ cups water

Sea salt and ground black pepper, to
taste

DIRECTIONS

- Press the "Sauté" button to preheat your Instant Pot. Once hot, heat the oil. Now, cook the garlic and scallions until tender.
- Add the remaining ingredients and stir to combine.
- Secure the lid. Choose the "Multigrain" mode and cook for 40 minutes under High pressure. Once cooking is complete, use a natural release; carefully remove the lid.
- Ladle into individual bowls and serve warm.

Per serving: 360 Calories; 6.4g Fat; 70g Carbs; 8.7g Protein; 2.2g Sugars

3. Savory Breakfast Quinoa

(Ready in about 10 minutes | Servings 4)

INGREDIENTS

2 teaspoons sesame oil

1 shallot, thinly sliced

2 bell peppers, thinly sliced

1 jalapeño pepper, seeded and sliced

1 teaspoon garlic, minced

Sea salt and ground black pepper, to taste

1/2 teaspoon mustard powder

1 teaspoon fennel seeds

1/2 teaspoon ground cumin

1 ½ cups quinoa, rinsed

1 ½ cups water

1 cup tomato purée

1 (15-ounce) can chickpeas, drained and rinsed

1 lime, cut into wedges

DIRECTIONS

- Press the "Sauté" button to preheat your Instant Pot. Heat the sesame oil. Then, sweat the shallot and peppers until they are tender and fragrant.
- Now, add the garlic, salt, black pepper, mustard powder, fennel seeds, cumin, quinoa, water, tomato purée, and chickpeas.
- Secure the lid. Choose the "Manual" mode and High pressure; cook for 1 minute. Once cooking is complete, use a natural pressure release; carefully remove the lid.
- Serve with fresh lime wedges. Bon appétit!

Per serving: 392 Calories; 8.1g Fat; 66.9g Carbs; 15.5g Protein; 7.9g Sugars

4. Aromatic Oats with Coconut

(Ready in about 15 minutes | Servings 2)

INGREDIENTS

4 cups water

1 ½ cups steel cut oats

1 tablespoon coconut oil

1/2 teaspoon cardamom

1/4 teaspoon grated nutmeg

1/2 teaspoon ground cinnamon

1/2 teaspoon vanilla essence

1/2 teaspoon ground star anise

1/2 cup coconut, flaked

DIRECTIONS

- Add water and oats to your Instant Pot.
- Secure the lid and choose the "Manual" mode. Cook for 10 minutes at High pressure.
- Once cooking is complete, use a quick release; remove the lid carefully. Add coconut oil and seasonings to the warm oatmeal and stir to combine well.
- Divide among individual bowls and serve topped with flaked coconut. Bon appétit!

Per serving: 243 Calories; 11.8g Fat; 48g Carbs; 12.6g Protein; 2.5g Sugars

5. Easy Porridge with Seeds and Nuts

(Ready in about 10 minutes | Servings 4)

INGREDIENTS

4 tablespoons shredded coconut, unsweetened
2 tablespoons pumpkin seeds
2 tablespoons flaxseed
1/2 cup almonds, chopped

1/2 teaspoon grated nutmeg
1/4 teaspoon ground cloves
1 teaspoon ground cinnamon
Himalayan salt, to taste
1 cup boiling water

DIRECTIONS

- Add all ingredients to the Instant Pot.
- Secure the lid. Choose "Manual" mode and High pressure; cook for 5 minutes. Once cooking is complete, use a quick pressure release; carefully remove the lid.
- Serve garnished with some extra slivered almonds if desired. Enjoy!

Per serving: 116 Calories; 10.5g Fat; 4.4g Carbs; 2.7g Protein; 0.8g Sugars

6. Rich Granola with Walnut

(Ready in about 2 hours 10 minutes | Servings 4)

INGREDIENTS

3/4 cup walnuts, soaked overnight and chopped

Himalayan salt, to taste

3/4 cup water

2 tablespoons coconut oil

1 tablespoon sunflower seeds

1/2 cup dried raspberries

1/2 teaspoon vanilla paste

1/4 teaspoon star anise, ground

1/4 teaspoon grated nutmeg

1/2 teaspoon ground cinnamon

DIRECTIONS

- Add all ingredients to your Instant Pot.
- Secure the lid. Choose "Slow Cook" mode and High pressure; cook for 2 hours. Once cooking is complete, use a quick pressure release; carefully remove the lid.
- Spoon into individual bowls and serve warm. Bon appétit!

Per serving: 199 Calories; 17.7g Fat; 9g Carbs; 3.1g Protein; 6.8g Sugars

7. Decadent Granola with Dark Rum

(Ready in about 2 hours 35 minutes | Servings 6)

INGREDIENTS

1 cup almonds

1 cup walnuts

2 ounces shredded coconut, unsweetened

1/4 cup sunflower seeds

1/4 cup pumpkin seeds

1 teaspoon vanilla paste

1/2 teaspoon ground cinnamon

A pinch of kosher salt

1/4 teaspoon star anise, ground

2 tablespoons dark rum

DIRECTIONS

- Place all ingredients in your Instant Pot.
- Secure the lid. Choose "Slow Cook" mode and High pressure; cook for 2 hours 30 minutes. Once cooking is complete, use a quick pressure release; carefully remove the lid.
- Spoon into individual bowls and serve warm. Bon appétit!

Per serving: 166 Calories; 14.2g Fat; 4.4g Carbs; 4.8g Protein; 0.9g Sugars

8. Romantic Autumn Porridge with Almonds

(Ready in about 10 minutes | Servings 2)

INGREDIENTS

2 tablespoons flaxseed meal

4 tablespoons coconut flour

1 tablespoon pumpkin seeds, chopped

1 tablespoon raw almonds, ground

1 cup unsweetened almond milk

1 cup water

1/8 teaspoon Monk fruit powder

DIRECTIONS

- Add all ingredients to the Instant Pot.
- Secure the lid. Choose "Manual" mode and High pressure; cook for 5 minutes. Once cooking is complete, use a quick pressure release; carefully remove the lid.
- Divide between two bowls and serve hot. Bon appétit!

Per serving: 308 Calories; 30.6g Fat; 7.9g Carbs; 5.6g Protein; 1.1g Sugars

9. Winter Noatmeal with Chia Seeds

(Ready in about 10 minutes | Servings 2)

INGREDIENTS

3 tablespoons pumpkin seeds

1 tablespoon chia seeds

1 tablespoon sunflower seeds

Himalayan salt, to taste

2 tablespoons coconut oil

1/2 cup coconut milk

1/2 cup water

1 teaspoon ground cinnamon

1 teaspoon vanilla paste

1/2 teaspoon granulated stevia

DIRECTIONS

- Place all ingredients in your Instant Pot.
- Secure the lid. Choose "Manual" mode and High pressure; cook for 5 minutes. Once cooking is complete, use a quick pressure release; carefully remove the lid.
- Divide between two bowls and serve hot. Bon appétit!

Per serving: 352 Calories; 34.8g Fat; 8.3g Carbs; 5.5g Protein; 2.4g Sugars

10. Easy Tofu Pâté

(Ready in about 10 minutes | Servings 8)

INGREDIENTS

3 tablespoons olive oil

2 yellow onions, peeled and sliced

1/2 teaspoon dried basil

1/2 teaspoon dried oregano

1 teaspoon dried thyme

2 garlic cloves, minced

1 cup tofu, pressed and cubed

1 tablespoon coconut aminos

Celery salt and ground black pepper, to taste

1 teaspoon smoked paprika

1/2 cup water

1/2 cup raw cashews, soaked overnight, drained

DIRECTIONS

- Press the "Sauté" button to heat up your Instant Pot. Heat the oil and sauté the onions until tender or about 2 minutes.
- Add the other ingredients, except for the cashews, and stir to combine well.
- Secure the lid. Choose "Manual" mode and High pressure; cook for 3 minutes. Once cooking is complete, use a quick pressure release; carefully remove the lid.
- Transfer the mixture to a food processor; stir in the cashews.
- Purée this mixture in your food processor, working in batches. Transfer to a nice serving bowl and serve with veggies for dipping. Bon appétit!

Per serving: 195 Calories; 16.3g Fat; 7.8g Carbs; 7.1g Protein; 2.1g Sugars

11. Broccoli and Mayo Pâté

(Ready in about 10 minutes | Servings 8)

INGREDIENTS

2 cups broccoli, cut into florets

2 ripe tomatoes, diced

1 yellow onion, chopped

2 garlic cloves, sliced

1 teaspoon fresh coriander, chopped

Seasoned salt, to taste

1/2 teaspoon ground black pepper

1/2 teaspoon cayenne pepper

1/2 teaspoon dried dill weed

1 teaspoon Ranch seasoning mix

1/2 cup vegan mayonnaise

DIRECTIONS

- Prepare your Instant Pot by adding 1 cup of water and a steamer basket to its bottom.
- Place the broccoli florets in the steamer basket.
- Secure the lid. Choose "Manual" mode and Low pressure; cook for 5 minutes. Once cooking is complete, use a quick pressure release; carefully remove the lid.
- Add the broccoli florets along with the remaining ingredients to your food processor. Process until everything is well incorporated.
- Serve well chilled with vegetable sticks. Bon appétit!

Per serving: 74 Calories; 6.1g Fat; 3.5g Carbs; 1.7g Protein; 1.5g Sugars

12. Tofu Scramble with Yemenite Hot Sauce (Zhoug)

(Ready in about 10 minutes | Servings 4)

INGREDIENTS

1 tablespoon grapeseed oil

1 (12-ounce) block extra-firm tofu, pressed and cubed

1/2 cup vegetable stock

1 teaspoon dried rosemary

Zhoug Sauce:

1 Hungarian wax pepper, stemmed and chopped

2 cloves garlic, chopped

1/2 cup fresh cilantro leaves

Kosher salt and ground black pepper, to taste

1/2 teaspoon ground cumin

1/3 cup extra-virgin olive oil

1 teaspoon sherry vinegar

DIRECTIONS

- Press the "Sauté" button to heat up your Instant Pot. Heat the oil until sizzling. Once hot, cook the tofu until it has begun to brown.
- Add vegetable stock and rosemary.
- Secure the lid. Choose "Manual" mode and High pressure; cook for 3 minutes. Once cooking is complete, use a quick pressure release; carefully remove the lid.
- Then, mix all ingredients for the sauce in your food processor. Store in your refrigerator until ready to use.
- Serve the tofu with the Zhoug sauce on the side. Enjoy!

Per serving: 308 Calories; 28.3g Fat; 4.5g Carbs; 12.3g Protein; 1.4g Sugars

SOUPS

13. Spicy Bean and Potato Soup

(Ready in about 30 minutes | Servings 4)

INGREDIENTS

2 tablespoons olive oil
2 onions, chopped
2 carrots chopped
2 parsnips, chopped
1 celery with leaves, chopped
2 Yukon gold potatoes, peeled and
   diced
2 ripe tomatoes, pureed
12 ounces Adzuki brans, soaked
   overnight

Kosher salt and ground black pepper,
   to taste
1 teaspoon cayenne pepper
1 teaspoon dried basil
1/2 teaspoon marjoram
1 teaspoon black garlic powder
1 teaspoon dried chive flakes
A few drops Sriracha
4 cups boiling water

DIRECTIONS

- Press the "Sauté" button to heat up the Instant Pot. Now, heat the olive oil and sweat the onions until just tender.
- Add the other ingredients; stir to combine well. Secure the lid and choose the "Manual" mode. Cook for 10 minutes at High Pressure.
- Once cooking is complete, use a natural release for 15 minutes; remove the lid carefully.
- Ladle into individual serving bowls and eat warm. Bon appétit!

Per serving: 474 Calories; 7.6g Fat; 84g Carbs; 20.5g Protein; 7.8g Sugars

14. Grandma's Vegetable and Noodle Soup

(Ready in about 20 minutes | Servings 6)

INGREDIENTS

2 tablespoons olive oil

2 shallots, peeled and chopped

1 carrot, chopped

1 parsnip, chopped

1 turnip, chopped

3 garlic cloves, smashed

1 teaspoon cumin powder

1/2 teaspoon dried rosemary

1/2 teaspoon dried thyme

6 cups vegetable stock, preferably
homemade

9 ounces vegan noodles

1 cup corn kernels

Salt and freshly ground black pepper,
to taste

DIRECTIONS

- Press the "Sauté" button to heat up your Instant Pot. Now, heat the oil and sauté the shallots with the carrot, parsnip, and turnip until they have softened.
- Stir in the garlic and cook an additional 40 seconds. Add the cumin powder, rosemary, thyme, stock, and noodles.
- Now, secure the lid and choose the "Soup" setting.
- Cook for 7 minutes at High pressure. Once cooking is complete, use a quick release; remove the lid carefully.
- Add the corn kernels, cover with the lid, and cook in the residual heat for 5 to 6 minutes more. Season with salt and pepper. Taste adjust the seasoning and serve warm. Bon appétit!

Per serving: 194 Calories; 5.4g Fat; 29.9g Carbs; 8g Protein; 5.1g Sugars

15. Aromatic Coconut Soup with Vegetables

(Ready in about 25 minutes | Servings 5)

INGREDIENTS

1 tablespoon olive oil
1/2 cup white onions, chopped
1 teaspoon garlic, minced
2 carrots, chopped
1 parsnip, chopped
1 celery, chopped
1 head cauliflower, cut into
   small florets

1 zucchini, diced
5 cups vegetable stock
Sea salt and ground black pepper, to
   taste
1/2 cup coconut cream
2 tablespoons fresh cilantro, chopped

DIRECTIONS

- Press the "Sauté" button to preheat your Instant Pot. Now, heat the oil until sizzling.
- Sauté the onion and garlic until tender. Add the carrots, parsnip, celery, cauliflower, zucchini, stock, salt, and black pepper, and stir to combine.
- Secure the lid. Choose the "Soup" mode and cook for 20 minutes under High pressure. Once cooking is complete, use a quick release; carefully remove the lid.
- Add coconut cream and seal the lid; let it sit until heated through. Ladle into soup bowls and serve garnished with fresh cilantro. Bon appétit!

Per serving: 176 Calories; 13.1g Fat; 9.3g Carbs; 7.9g Protein; 3.4g Sugars

16. Easy Russian Borscht

(Ready in about 15 minutes | Servings 4)

INGREDIENTS

1 ½ tablespoons olive oil

1/2 cup onions, chopped

2 garlic cloves, pressed

Kosher salt and ground black pepper,
   to taste

1/2 pound potatoes, peeled and diced

2 carrots, chopped

1/2 pound beets, peeled and coarsely
   shredded

2 tablespoons red-wine vinegar

1 tomato, chopped

4 cups vegetable stock

1/2 teaspoon caraway seeds

1/4 cup fresh dill, roughly chopped

DIRECTIONS

- Press the "Sauté" button to preheat your Instant Pot. Heat the oil and cook the onions and garlic until tender and fragrant.
- Add the remaining ingredients, except for the fresh dill.
- Secure the lid. Choose the "Manual" mode and cook for 10 minutes under High pressure. Once cooking is complete, use a natural release; carefully remove the lid.
- Serve the soup with chopped fresh dill. Enjoy!

Per serving: 183 Calories; 7.3g Fat; 22.5g Carbs; 8.4g Protein; 7.7g Sugars

17. Spanish-Style Tomato Soup

(Ready in about 15 minutes | Servings 4)

INGREDIENTS

2 tablespoons olive oil

1/2 cup green onions, chopped

2 cloves garlic, crushed

2 carrots, roughly chopped

1 red chili pepper, seeded and
   chopped

1 pound ripe tomatoes, puréed

1 zucchini, chopped

1 teaspoon dried rosemary

1/2 teaspoon dried basil

1/2 teaspoon dried marjoram

1 teaspoon sweet paprika

Sea salt and ground black pepper, to
   taste

1 cup vegetable stock

2 tablespoons fresh chives, chopped

2 tablespoons pepitas

DIRECTIONS

- Press the "Sauté" button to preheat your Instant Pot. Then, heat the oil until sizzling.
- Now, cook the green onions and garlic until tender and fragrant. Add carrots, chili pepper, tomatoes, zucchini, seasonings, and stock.
- Secure the lid. Choose the "Manual" mode and cook for 6 minutes under High pressure. Once cooking is complete, use a quick release; carefully remove the lid.
- Then, purée the mixture with an immersion blender until the desired thickness is reached.
- Ladle into soup bowls; serve garnished with fresh chives and pepitas. Enjoy!

Per serving: 125 Calories; 9.4g Fat; 8.1g Carbs; 4.2g Protein; 1.8g Sugars

18. Asian-Style Spicy Soup

(Ready in about 35 minutes | Servings 4)

INGREDIENTS

1 tablespoon toasted sesame oil

1 yellow onion, peeled and chopped

2 garlic cloves, minced

1 teaspoon fresh ginger, peeled and grated

1 jalapeño pepper, minced

1 celery stalk, chopped

2 carrots, chopped

1 teaspoon Five-spice powder

Sea salt, to taste

1/2 teaspoon ground black pepper, to taste

1/2 teaspoon red pepper flakes

1 teaspoon dried parsley flakes

4 cups vegetable broth

2 ripe tomatoes, finely chopped

1 tablespoon soy sauce

1 cup sweet corn kernels, frozen and thawed

1 cup zha cai

DIRECTIONS

- Press the "Sauté" button to preheat your Instant Pot. Once hot, add the oil. Sauté the onion, garlic, ginger and jalapeño pepper for 2 to 3 minutes, stirring occasionally.
- Add the remaining ingredients, except for corn and zha cai; stir to combine well.
- Secure the lid. Choose the "Bean/Chili" mode and cook for 25 minutes under High pressure. Once cooking is complete, use a natural release; carefully remove the lid.
- After that, add corn and seal the lid again. Let it sit until heated through. Serve in individual bowls with zha cai on the side. Enjoy!

Per serving: 177 Calories; 8.8g Fat; 18.5g Carbs; 7.8g Protein; 7.1g Sugars

19. Mushroom Soup with Rice Noodles

(Ready in about 25 minutes | Servings 6)

INGREDIENTS

6 cups vegan cream of mushroom
 soup
1/2 teaspoon dried basil
1 teaspoon dried oregano
1 teaspoon dried parsley flakes
1 teaspoon fennel seeds
2 carrots, thinly sliced
1 celery stalk, chopped
1 parsnip, chopped
1 red onion, chopped

2 cloves garlic, minced
1 cup brown mushrooms, chopped
2 cups rice noodles
1/2 tablespoon miso paste
1/2 teaspoon freshly ground black
 pepper
1/4 teaspoon red pepper flakes,
 crushed
Salt, to taste

DIRECTIONS

- Place the cream of mushroom soup, basil, oregano, parsley, fennel seeds, carrots, celery, parsnip, onion, garlic, mushrooms in your Instant Pot.
- Secure the lid. Choose the "Soup" mode and cook for 8 minutes under High pressure. Once cooking is complete, use a natural release; carefully remove the lid.
- Add the rice noodles, miso paste, black pepper, red pepper, and salt to the Instant Pot.
- Press the "Sauté" button and cook an additional 7 to 10 minutes. Ladle into individual bowls and serve right away!

Per serving: 292 Calories; 13.7g Fat; 37.7g Carbs; 5.5g Protein; 3.1g Sugars

20. Soup with Vegetables with Wild Rice

(Ready in about 35 minutes | Servings 4)

INGREDIENTS

2 tablespoons olive oil

1/2 cup leeks, roughly chopped

2 garlic cloves, minced

1 bell pepper, chopped

1 serrano pepper, chopped

2 carrots, chopped

1 fennel, diced

3/4 cup wild rice

1 cup tomato purée

2 cups water

2 cups vegetable broth

2 tablespoons fresh coriander, chopped

1 teaspoon fresh or dried rosemary

Salt, to taste

1/2 teaspoon ground black pepper

DIRECTIONS

- Press the "Sauté" button to preheat your Instant Pot. Once hot, heat the oil.
- Then, sauté the leeks, garlic, and pepper for 2 to 4 minutes, stirring periodically; add a splash of broth if needed.
- Stir the remaining ingredients into your Instant Pot; stir to combine well.
- Secure the lid. Choose the "Soup" mode and High pressure; cook for 30 minutes. Once cooking is complete, use a natural pressure release; carefully remove the lid.
- Taste and adjust the seasonings; ladle into soup bowls and serve hot. Enjoy!

Per serving: 235 Calories; 8.1g Fat; 34.2g Carbs; 8.6g Protein; 6.3g Sugars

21. Creamed Peppery Soup with Almond Milk

(Ready in about 15 minutes | Servings 4)

INGREDIENTS

3 teaspoons sesame oil

1/2 cup leeks, chopped

1 garlic clove, minced

1 celery with leaves, chopped

1 carrot, trimmed and chopped

1 red bell pepper, thinly sliced

1 green bell pepper, thinly sliced

1 serrano pepper, deveined and thinly sliced

4 ½ cups water

Salt and ground black pepper, to taste

1 tablespoon soy sauce

1/2 cup raw cashews, soaked for 3 hours

1/2 cup almond milk, unsweetened

DIRECTIONS

- Press the "Sauté" button on your Instant Pot. Heat the sesame oil and sauté the leeks until they are just tender.
- Add garlic, celery, carrot, and peppers; continue sautéing until they have softened, about 3 minutes.
- Add water, salt, and pepper. Choose the "Manual" mode and cook for 4 minutes at High pressure.
- Once cooking is complete, use a quick release; remove the lid carefully.
- Next, puree the soy sauce, raw cashews, and almond milk in your food processor or blender; process until creamy and uniform.
- Stir this cream base into the soup; cook in the residual heat until everything is well incorporated.
- Divide the warm chowder among individual serving bowls. Side with crackers and enjoy!

Per serving: 282 Calories; 22.2g Fat; 18.4g Carbs; 6.1g Protein; 7.9g Sugars

22. Cream of Mushroom Soup with Asparagus

(Ready in about 15 minutes | Servings 4)

INGREDIENTS

2 tablespoons coconut oil

1/2 cup shallots, chopped

2 cloves garlic, minced

1 pound asparagus, washed, trimmed
    and chopped

4 ounces button mushrooms, sliced

4 cups vegetable broth

2 tablespoons balsamic vinegar

Himalayan salt, to taste

1/4 teaspoon ground black pepper

1/4 teaspoon paprika

1/4 cup vegan sour cream

DIRECTIONS

- Press the "Sauté" button to heat up your Instant Pot. Heat the oil and cook the shallots and garlic for 2 to 3 minutes.
- Add the remaining ingredients, except for sour cream, to the Instant Pot.
- Secure the lid. Choose "Manual" mode and High pressure; cook for 4 minutes. Once cooking is complete, use a quick pressure release; carefully remove the lid.
- Spoon into four soup bowls; add a dollop of sour cream to each serving and serve immediately. Bon appétit!

Per serving: 171 Calories; 11.7g Fat; 9.2g Carbs; 9.7g Protein; 3.4g Sugars

24. Rich Garden Vegetable Soup

(Ready in about 10 minutes | Servings 4)

INGREDIENTS

1 ½ tablespoons olive oil

1 leek, chopped

2 cloves garlic, smashed

1 parsnip, chopped

1 celery stalk, chopped

4 cups water

2 bouillon cubes

1/2 pound green cabbage, shredded

1 zucchini, sliced

2 bay leaves

1/2 teaspoon ground cumin

1/2 teaspoon turmeric powder

1 teaspoon dried basil

Kosher salt and ground black pepper, to taste

6 ounces Swiss chard

DIRECTIONS

- Press the "Sauté" button to heat up your Instant Pot. Heat the olive oil and cook the leek for 2 to 3 minutes or until it has softened.
- Add the other ingredients, except for the Swiss chard, to the Instant Pot; stir to combine well.
- Secure the lid. Choose "Manual" mode and High pressure; cook for 3 minutes. Once cooking is complete, use a quick pressure release; carefully remove the lid.
- Add the Swiss chard and cover with the lid. Allow it to sit in the residual heat until it is wilted.
- Discard bay leaves and ladle into soup bowls. Serve warm and enjoy!

Per serving: 99 Calories; 5.5g Fat; 9.2g Carbs; 2g Protein; 3.4g Sugars

25. Light Zucchini Soup with Coriander

(Ready in about 15 minutes | Servings 4)

INGREDIENTS

2 tablespoons coconut oil

1 medium-sized leek, thinly sliced

1 zucchini, chopped

2 garlic cloves, crushed

Sea salt and ground black pepper, to
your liking

1/2 teaspoon cayenne pepper

4 cups vegetable stock

1/4 cup coriander leaves, chopped

DIRECTIONS

- Press the "Sauté" button to heat up your Instant Pot. Heat the coconut oil and sauté the leeks, zucchini, and garlic.
- Next, stir in the salt, black pepper, cayenne pepper, and stock.
- Secure the lid. Choose "Manual" mode and High pressure; cook for 8 minutes. Once cooking is complete, use a natural pressure release; carefully remove the lid.
- Serve warm garnished with coriander leaves. Bon appétit!

Per serving: 90 Calories; 7.4g Fat; 4.9g Carbs; 2g Protein; 1.5g Sugars

MAIN COURSE

26. Smoked Risotto with Herbs

(Ready in about 15 minutes | Servings 2)

INGREDIENTS

1 tablespoon olive oil

2 garlic cloves, minced

1 white onion, finely chopped

1 cup Arborio rice

1 cup water

1 cup vegetable stock

1/2 teaspoon dried basil

1/2 teaspoon dried oregano

Sea salt and ground black pepper, to taste

1 teaspoon smoked paprika

DIRECTIONS

- Press the "Sauté" button to preheat your Instant Pot. Heat the oil and sauté the garlic and onion until tender and fragrant or about 3 minutes.
- Add the remaining ingredients; stir to combine well.
- Secure the lid. Choose the "Manual" mode and cook for 5 minutes under High pressure. Once cooking is complete, use a quick release; carefully remove the lid.
- Ladle into individual bowls and serve warm. Enjoy!

Per serving: 291 Calories; 20g Fat; 35.4g Carbs; 11.3g Protein; 2.8g Sugars

27. Sunday Quinoa with Mushrooms

(Ready in about 15 minutes | Servings 4)

INGREDIENTS

2 cups dry quinoa

3 cups water

2 tablespoons olive oil

1 onion, chopped

1 bell pepper, chopped

2 garlic cloves, chopped

2 cups Cremini mushrooms, thinly sliced

1/2 teaspoon sea salt

1/3 teaspoon ground black pepper, or more to taste

1 teaspoon cayenne pepper

1/2 teaspoon dried dill

1/4 teaspoon ground bay leaf

DIRECTIONS

- Add the quinoa and water to your Instant Pot.
- Secure the lid. Choose the "Manual" mode and cook for 1 minute under High pressure. Once cooking is complete, use a natural release; carefully remove the lid.
- Drain the quinoa and set it aside.
- Press the "Sauté" button to preheat your Instant Pot. Once hot, heat the oil. Then, sauté the onion until tender and translucent.
- Add bell pepper, garlic, and mushrooms and continue to sauté for 1 to 2 minutes more or until they are fragrant. Stir the remaining ingredients into your Instant Pot.
- Add the reserved quinoa and stir to combine well. Serve warm. Bon appétit!

Per serving: 401 Calories; 12.1g Fat; 60.2g Carbs; 14.1g Protein; 2.7g Sugars

28. Traditional Chili with Tortilla Chips

(Ready in about 15 minutes | Servings 6)

INGREDIENTS

2 tablespoons olive oil

1 red onion, chopped

3 cloves garlic minced or pressed

1 red bell pepper, diced

1 green bell pepper, diced

1 red chili pepper, minced

Sea salt and ground black pepper, to taste

1 teaspoon cayenne pepper

1/2 teaspoon ground cumin

2 cups vegetable stock

2 ripe tomatoes, chopped

2 (15-ounce) cans beans, drained and rinsed

1 handful fresh cilantro leaves, chopped

1/2 cup tortilla chips

DIRECTIONS

- Press the "Sauté" button to preheat your Instant Pot. Now, heat the oil until sizzling.
- Sauté the onion tender and translucent. Add garlic, peppers, salt, and pepper; continue to sauté until they are tender.
- Now, stir in the cayenne pepper, cumin, stock, tomatoes, and beans.
- Secure the lid. Choose the "Manual" mode and cook for 10 minutes under High pressure. Once cooking is complete, use a quick release; carefully remove the lid.
- Divide the chili between six serving bowls; top with fresh cilantro and tortilla chips. Enjoy!

Per serving: 204 Calories; 6.5g Fat; 27.9g Carbs; 10.4g Protein; 6.9g Sugars

29. Green Beans with Mushrooms and Scallions

(Ready in about 25 minutes | Servings 4)

INGREDIENTS

2 cups water

6 dried shiitake mushrooms

2 tablespoons sesame oil

2 cloves garlic, minced

1/2 cup scallions, chopped

1 ½ pounds green beans, fresh or frozen (and thawed)

1/4 teaspoon ground black pepper

1/2 teaspoon red pepper flakes, crushed

1 bay leaf

Sea salt, to taste

DIRECTIONS

- Press the "Sauté" button and bring the water to a rapid boil; remove from the heat; add the dried shiitake mushrooms.
- Allow the mushrooms to sit for 15 minutes to rehydrate. Then cut the mushrooms into slices; reserve the mushroom stock.
- Wipe down the Instant Pot with a kitchen cloth. Press the "Sauté" button to preheat your Instant Pot. Once hot, heat the sesame oil.
- Then, sauté the garlic and scallions until tender and aromatic. Add the green beans, black pepper, red pepper, bay leaf, salt, reserved mushrooms and stock; stir to combine well.
- Secure the lid. Choose the "Manual" mode and cook for 4 minutes under High pressure. Once cooking is complete, use a quick release; carefully remove the lid. Serve warm.

Per serving: 119 Calories; 7.6g Fat; 12.6g Carbs; 2.6g Protein; 2.6g Sugars

30. Red Lentil with Tomatoes and Cilantro

(Ready in about 20 minutes | Servings 4)

INGREDIENTS

1 tablespoon olive oil

2 cups red lentils

1/2 cup scallions, finely chopped

1 teaspoon garlic, minced

1 teaspoon turmeric powder

Sea salt and ground black pepper, to
taste

1 teaspoon sweet paprika

1 (15-ounce) can tomatoes, crushed

1 bay leaf

1 handful fresh cilantro leaves,
chopped

DIRECTIONS

- Add the olive oil, lentils, scallions, garlic, turmeric, salt, black pepper, paprika, tomatoes, and bay leaf to your Instant Pot.
- Secure the lid. Choose the "Manual" mode and cook for 12 minutes under High pressure. Once cooking is complete, use a natural release; carefully remove the lid.
- Discard the bay leaf and spoon lentil into serving bowls. Serve topped with fresh cilantro. Enjoy!

Per serving: 405 Calories; 5.9g Fat; 67.5g Carbs; 24.5g Protein; 3.8g Sugars

31. Penne Pasta with Tomato-Sherry Sauce

(Ready in about 15 minutes | Servings 4)

INGREDIENTS

1 tablespoon canola oil

1 small-sized leek, chopped

1 teaspoon garlic, smashed

1 ¼ pounds penne pasta

4 ripe tomatoes, pureed

2 cups roasted vegetable stock, preferably homemade

1 teaspoon dried rosemary

1/2 teaspoon dried oregano

1/2 teaspoon daikon radish seeds

A pinch of sugar

Sea salt and freshly ground black pepper, to your liking

1 teaspoon cayenne pepper

1/3 cup dry sherry

DIRECTIONS

- Press the "Sauté" button to heat up your Instant Pot. When hot, add the canola oil and sauté the leeks and garlic until aromatic.
- Stir in penne, tomatoes, and roasted vegetable stock. Now, add the other ingredients and secure the lid. Choose the "Manual" function and cook for 6 minutes under High pressure.
- Once cooking is complete, use a natural release; remove the lid carefully.
- Divide among four serving bowls and serve garnished with vegan parmesan.
  Bon appétit!

Per serving: 281 Calories; 5g Fat; 54g Carbs; 7.6g Protein; 8.8g Sugars

32. Rice with Purple Cabbage

(Ready in about 25 minutes | Servings 4)

INGREDIENTS

2 tablespoons olive oil

2 shallots, diced

1 garlic clove, minced

1 head purple cabbage, cut into
   wedges

2 ripe tomatoes, pureed

2 tablespoons tomato ketchup

1 cup basmati rice

1 ½ cups water

1 bay leaf

1/4 teaspoon marjoram

1/2 teaspoon cayenne pepper

Salt and freshly ground black pepper,
   to taste

1/4 cup fresh chives, chopped

DIRECTIONS

- Press the "Sauté" button to preheat the Instant Pot. Heat the olive oil and sauté the shallots until they are just tender.
- Now, stir in the minced garlic and cook until it is lightly browned and aromatic.
- Stir in the cabbage, tomatoes, ketchup, rice, water, bay leaf, marjoram, cayenne pepper, salt, and black pepper.
- Secure the lid. Select the "Manual" mode and cook for 6 minutes under High pressure. Once cooking is complete, use a natural release for 15 minutes; remove the lid carefully. Serve warm garnished with fresh chopped chives. Bon appétit!

Per serving: 242 Calories; 13.3g Fat; 35.2g Carbs; 7.8g Protein; 10g Sugars

33. Country-Style Lentil Stew

(Ready in about 15 minutes | Servings 4)

INGREDIENTS

2 teaspoons toasted sesame oil
1 yellow onion, chopped
2 cloves garlic, pressed
1 teaspoon fresh ginger, grated
1 bell pepper, chopped
1 serrano pepper, chopped
1/2 teaspoon ground allspice
1/2 teaspoon ground cumin
1/2 teaspoon dried basil

1 teaspoon dried parsley flakes
Sea salt and black pepper, to taste
1 ½ cups tomato purée
2 cups vegetable stock
1 cup beluga lentils
2 cups kale leaves, torn into pieces
1 teaspoon fresh lemon juice
1/2 cup cashew cream

DIRECTIONS

- Press the "Sauté" button to preheat your Instant Pot. Now, heat the oil; sauté the onion until tender and translucent.
- Then, add the garlic, ginger, and peppers; continue to sauté until they have softened.
- Add the seasonings, tomato purée, stock and lentils.
- Secure the lid. Choose the "Manual" mode and High pressure; cook for 8 minutes. Once cooking is complete, use a natural pressure release; carefully remove the lid.
- Add the kale and lemon juice; seal the lid again and let it sit until thoroughly warmed. Serve dolloped with cashew cream. Enjoy!

Per serving: 311 Calories; 22.9g Fat; 21.8g Carbs; 9.9g Protein; 6.7g Sugars

34. Aromatic Chili with Sweet Potatoes and Rum

(Ready in about 25 minutes | Servings 4)

INGREDIENTS

2 tablespoons sesame oil

1/2 cup red onion, sliced

2 cloves garlic crushed

1 roasted bell pepper, cut into strips

1 teaspoon habanero pepper, minced

1 pound sweet potatoes, peeled and
  cut into bite-sized chunks

1 cup vegetable broth

1 cup water

Sea salt, to taste

1 teaspoon black peppercorns, crushed

1/4 teaspoon allspice

1/8 teaspoon ground clove

1 teaspoon sweet paprika

1/2 teaspoon smoked paprika

1 pound red kidney beans, soaked
  overnight and well-rinsed

1/2 (15-ounce) can tomatoes, diced

1/4 cup rum

1 (7-ounce) can salsa verde

DIRECTIONS

- Press the "Sauté" button to preheat your Instant Pot. Now, heat the oil; sauté the onion until tender and translucent or about 2 minutes.
- Then, stir in the garlic and peppers; continue to sauté for a further 2 minutes. Now, add the sweet potatoes, broth, water, spices, beans, and tomatoes.
- Secure the lid. Choose the "Bean/Chili" mode and High pressure; cook for 15 minutes. Once cooking is complete, use a natural pressure release; carefully remove the lid.
- Add the rum and salsa verde. Press the "Sauté" button and continue to cook until everything is thoroughly heated. Enjoy!

Per serving: 300 Calories; 11.4g Fat; 36.1g Carbs; 8.3g Protein; 7.9g Sugars

35. One-Pot Italian Lasagne

(Ready in about 25 minutes | Servings 4)

INGREDIENTS

2 teaspoons canola oil

1 red onion, chopped

2 cloves garlic, minced

2 carrots chopped

2 bell peppers, chopped

1/2 cup French green lentils, well-rinsed

2 ripe tomatoes, puréed

1 tablespoon Italian seasoning

Sea salt and ground black pepper, to taste

1 teaspoon red pepper flakes, crushed

1 cup water

1 cup vegetable stock

6 ounces lasagna sheets, broken into small pieces

1/2 cup vegan mozzarella, to serve

DIRECTIONS

- Press the "Sauté" button to preheat your Instant Pot. Now, heat the oil and cook the onion until tender and translucent.
- Now, add the garlic and continue to sauté it for 30 seconds more.
- Add the carrots, peppers, lentils, tomatoes, seasonings, water vegetable stock, and lasagna sheets.
- Secure the lid. Choose the "Manual" mode and High pressure; cook for 10 minutes. Once cooking is complete, use a natural pressure release for 10 minutes; carefully remove the lid.
- Serve with vegan mozzarella. Bon appétit!

Per serving: 269 Calories; 3.9g Fat; 49.2g Carbs; 11.8g Protein; 6.4g Sugars

36. Rustic Mushroom and Potato Stew

(Ready in about 25 minutes | Servings 4)

INGREDIENTS

1 pound russet potatoes, peeled and diced

3/4 pound chanterelle mushrooms, sliced

1 tablespoon olive oil

1 carrot, chopped

1 parsnip, chopped

1 yellow onion, chopped

2 cloves garlic, peeled and minced

2 sprigs fresh rosemary

2 sprigs fresh thyme

1 teaspoon red chili flakes

2 tablespoons fresh parsley, chopped

2 cups vegetable stock

1/3 cup port wine

1 ripe Roma tomato, chopped

Sea salt and ground black pepper, to taste

1 tablespoon paprika

1 tablespoon flax seeds meal

DIRECTIONS

- Throw all ingredients, except for the flax seeds meal, in your Instant Pot.
- Secure the lid. Choose the "Soup" mode and High pressure; cook for 20 minutes. Once cooking is complete, use a natural pressure release; carefully remove the lid.
- Stir the flax seeds into your Instant Pot. Press the "Sauté" button and let it simmer until cooking liquid has thickened and reduced. Serve hot. Bon appétit!

Per serving: 456 Calories; 5.7g Fat; 99g Carbs; 15.4g Protein; 7.9g Sugars

37. Spicy Lentil Gumbo

(Ready in about 15 minutes | Servings 4)

INGREDIENTS

2 tablespoons sesame oil

1 shallot, chopped

3 cloves garlic, minced

1 teaspoon jalapeño pepper, minced

1 celery stalk, chopped

1 carrot, chopped

1 parsnip, chopped

1/2 teaspoon dried basil

1 teaspoon dried parsley flakes

1 teaspoon red pepper flakes, crushed

1 1/3 cups lentils, regular

4 cups vegetable broth

1 ½ cups fresh or frozen chopped okra

2 ripe tomatoes, chopped

Salt, to taste

1/2 teaspoon ground black pepper

1 teaspoon light brown sugar

DIRECTIONS

- Press the "Sauté" button to preheat the Instant Pot. Heat the oil and now, sauté the shallot until tender and fragrant.
- After that, stir in garlic; cook an additional 30 seconds or until aromatic. Then, stir in the remaining ingredients.
- Secure the lid. Choose the "Manual" mode and High pressure; cook for 12 minutes. Once cooking is complete, use a natural pressure release; carefully remove the lid.
- Taste, adjust the seasonings and serve warm. Bon appétit!

Per serving: 196 Calories; 8.8g Fat; 22.7g Carbs; 9.6g Protein; 7.7g Sugars

38. Kidney Beans with Roasted Peppers

(Ready in about 30 minutes | Servings 4)

INGREDIENTS

1 pound dried red kidney beans

1/2 cup shallots, chopped

2 cloves garlic, chopped

2 roasted peppers, cut into strips

1 teaspoon ground cumin

1/2 teaspoon mustard powder

1 teaspoon celery seeds

Sea salt and ground black pepper, to taste

2 cups roasted vegetable broth

DIRECTIONS

- Add all of the above ingredients to your Instant Pot.
- Secure the lid. Choose the "Bean/Chili" mode and cook for 25 minutes under High pressure. Once cooking is complete, use a natural release; carefully remove the lid.
- You can thicken the cooking liquid on "Sauté" function if desired. Serve warm.

Per serving: 418 Calories; 2.1g Fat; 72.9g Carbs; 30.1g Protein; 4.5g Sugars

VEGETABLES & SIDE DISHES

39. Bean Salad with Peppers

(Ready in about 35 minutes + chilling time | Servings 4)

INGREDIENTS

1 cup Great Northern beans

6 cups water

1 cucumber, peeled and sliced

1 red bell pepper, seeded and chopped

1 green bell pepper, seeded and chopped

1 teaspoon ground sumac

3 tablespoons extra-virgin olive oil

1 tablespoon fresh lime juice

1/4 cup fresh parsley leaves, roughly chopped

1/4 teaspoon freshly ground black pepper

1/2 teaspoon red pepper flakes

Salt, to taste

DIRECTIONS

- Place the beans and water in your Instant Pot.
- Secure the lid. Choose the "Bean/Chili" mode and cook for 30 minutes under High pressure. Once cooking is complete, use a natural release; carefully remove the lid.
- Allow the prepared beans to cool completely. Now, add the remaining ingredients to the Instant Pot.
- Toss to combine and serve well chilled. Enjoy!

Per serving: 207 Calories; 5.1g Fat; 31.2g Carbs; 10.6g Protein; 2.3g Sugars

40. Asparagus Salad with Romano Cheese

(Ready in about 10 minutes | Servings 4)

INGREDIENTS

1 pound asparagus, trimmed

2 tomatoes, diced

4 tablespoons olive oil

1 shallot, chopped

1 teaspoon garlic, minced

Sea salt and ground black pepper, to
taste

2 tablespoons lemon juice

1 tablespoon Dijon mustard

1/2 cup Romano cheese, grated

1 handful Italian parsley

DIRECTIONS

- Add 1 cup of water and a metal trivet to the Instant Pot. Place the asparagus on the trivet.
- Secure the lid. Choose the "Manual" mode and cook for 1 minute under High pressure. Once cooking is complete, use a quick release; carefully remove the lid.
- Toss the prepared asparagus with the remaining ingredients; toss to combine well. Place in your refrigerator until ready to serve. Enjoy!

Per serving: 230 Calories; 19.1g Fat; 10.1g Carbs; 7.9g Protein; 4.9g Sugars

41. Steamed Vegetables with Peanut Sauce

(Ready in about 10 minutes | Servings 4)

INGREDIENTS

1 ¼ cups water

1 pound broccoli florets

1 carrot, diced

1/2 teaspoon sea salt

1/2 teaspoon cayenne pepper

1/4 teaspoon ground white pepper

For the Sauce:

4 tablespoons silky peanut butter

3 tablespoons water

1 tablespoon champagne vinegar

1 tablespoons poppy seeds

DIRECTIONS

- Add 1 ¼ cups of water to the base of your Instant Pot. Arrange the broccoli and carrots in a steaming basket and transfer them to the Instant Pot.
- Secure the lid, choose the "Manual" mode, and cook for 3 minutes at High pressure. Once cooking is complete, use a quick release; carefully remove the lid.
- Season your vegetables with salt, cayenne pepper, and ground white pepper.
- Meanwhile, in a mixing bowl, thoroughly combine the peanut butter, water, vinegar, and poppy seeds.
- Serve the steamed broccoli and carrots with the peanut sauce on the side. Bon appétit!

Per serving: 90 Calories; 4.3g Fat; 9.3g Carbs; 5.2g Protein; 4.3g Sugars

42. Curried Cabbage with Winter Vegetables

(Ready in about 20 minutes | Servings 4)

INGREDIENTS

2 tablespoons olive oil

1 medium-sized leek, chopped

2 cloves garlic, smashed

1 ½ pounds white cabbage, shredded

1 cup vegetable broth

1 cup tomatoes, puréed

1 parsnip, chopped

2 carrots, chopped

2 stalks celery, chopped

1 turnip, chopped

1/2 tablespoon fresh lime juice

1 teaspoon dried basil

1/2 teaspoon dried dill

1 teaspoon ground coriander

1 teaspoon ground turmeric

1 bay leaf

Kosher salt and ground black pepper, to taste

1 (14-ounce) can coconut milk

DIRECTIONS

- Press the "Sauté" button to preheat your Instant Pot. Now, heat the oil and cook the leeks and garlic until tender and fragrant.
- After that, add the remaining ingredients; stir to combine well.
- Secure the lid. Choose the "Manual" mode and cook for 12 minutes under High pressure. Once cooking is complete, use a natural release; carefully remove the lid.
- Ladle into soup bowls and serve immediately.

Per serving: 223 Calories; 8.2g Fat; 33.8g Carbs; 7.6g Protein; 15.1g Sugars

43. Brussels Sprouts with Tomato and Cashews

(Ready in about 15 minutes | Servings 4)

INGREDIENTS

1 pound Brussels sprouts, cut into
   halves
1/2 cup water
1/2 cup tomato purée
Salt and ground black pepper, to taste
1/2 teaspoon cayenne pepper or more
   to taste

2 tablespoons soy sauce
1 fresh lime juice
1/4 cup cashew nuts, chopped
1/4 cup fresh cilantro leaves, chopped

DIRECTIONS

- Add the Brussels sprouts, water, tomato purée, salt, black pepper, and cayenne pepper to the Instant Pot.
- Secure the lid. Choose the "Manual" mode and cook for 4 minutes under High pressure. Once cooking is complete, use a quick release; carefully remove the lid.
- Drizzle soy sauce and lime juice over the top. Add cashew nuts and fresh cilantro leaves. Serve immediately.

Per serving: 132 Calories; 5.7g Fat; 17.8g Carbs; 6.3g Protein; 5.9g Sugars

44. Vegan Dum Aloo

(Ready in about 15 minutes | Servings 6)

INGREDIENTS

1 tablespoon canola oil

1/2 cup scallions, chopped

2 cloves garlic, minced

1 teaspoon red chili pepper, minced

2 pounds baby potatoes, diced

1 tablespoon curry paste

1 cup water

1 cup vegetable broth

1 cup full-fat coconut milk

Salt, to taste

1/2 teaspoon ground black pepper

1 teaspoon cayenne pepper

1 teaspoon cumin

DIRECTIONS

- Press the "Sauté" button to preheat your Instant Pot. Now, heat the canola oil until sizzling; sauté the scallions until just tender.
- Add garlic and chili pepper; allow it to cook an additional 30 seconds, stirring continuously. Add the remaining ingredients.
- Secure the lid. Choose the "Manual" mode and High pressure; cook for 5 minutes. Once cooking is complete, use a quick pressure release; carefully remove the lid. Serve hot.

Per serving: 246 Calories; 12.4g Fat; 31.1g Carbs; 5.3g Protein; 3.1g Sugars

45. Mashed Potatoes with Soy Milk

(Ready in about 15 minutes | Servings 6)

INGREDIENTS

2 pounds potatoes, peeled and diced

3 garlic cloves, peeled

1 cup vegetable stock

Salt, to taste

1/3 teaspoon ground black pepper

A pinch of grated nutmeg

4 tablespoons vegan butter, softened

2 tablespoons soy milk

1 teaspoon paprika powder

DIRECTIONS

- Add the potatoes, garlic, stock, salt, pepper, nutmeg and butter to your Instant Pot.
- Secure the lid. Choose the "Manual" mode and High pressure; cook for 5 minutes. Once cooking is complete, use a quick pressure release; carefully remove the lid.
- Then, purée the mixture with a potato masher; add the soy milk and continue to mash until your desired texture is reached.
- Sprinkle paprika over the top and serve warm. Bon appétit!

Per serving: 196 Calories; 8.3g Fat; 27.2g Carbs; 4.2g Protein; 1.4g Sugars

46. Zucchini with Garlic and Herbs

(Ready in about 10 minutes | Servings 4)

INGREDIENTS

1 ½ tablespoons olive oil

2 garlic cloves, minced

1 ½ pounds zucchinis, sliced

1/2 cup vegetable broth

Salt and pepper, to taste

1/2 teaspoon dried rosemary

1 teaspoon dried basil

1/2 teaspoon smoked paprika

DIRECTIONS

- Press the "Sauté" button to heat up your Instant Pot. Now, heat the olive oil and cook the garlic until aromatic.
- Add the remaining ingredients.
- Secure the lid. Choose "Manual" mode and Low pressure; cook for 3 minutes. Once cooking is complete, use a quick pressure release; carefully remove the lid. Bon appétit!

Per serving: 88 Calories; 5.9g Fat; 5.1g Carbs; 5.3g Protein; 0.1g Sugars

47. Spicy Green Cabbage with Rice Wine

(Ready in about 10 minutes | Servings 4)

INGREDIENTS

2 tablespoons olive oil

1/2 cup yellow onion, sliced

1 teaspoon garlic, smashed

Sea salt and freshly ground black pepper, to taste

1 teaspoon turmeric powder

1 serrano pepper, chopped

1 pound green cabbage, shredded

1 celery stalk, chopped

2 tablespoons rice wine

1 cup roasted vegetable broth

DIRECTIONS

- Place all of the above ingredients in the Instant Pot.
- Secure the lid. Choose "Manual" mode and High pressure; cook for 4 minutes. Once cooking is complete, use a quick pressure release; carefully remove the lid.
- Divide between individual bowls and serve warm. Bon appétit!

Per serving: 114 Calories; 8.4g Fat; 8.1g Carbs; 2.8g Protein; 4.3g Sugars

48. Easy Masala Cauliflower

(Ready in about 10 minutes | Servings 4)

INGREDIENTS

2 tablespoons grapeseed oil

1/2 cup scallions, chopped

2 cloves garlic, pressed

1 tablespoon garam masala

1 teaspoon curry powder

1 red chili pepper, minced

1/2 teaspoon ground cumin

Sea salt and ground black pepper, to taste

1 tablespoon fresh coriander, chopped

1 teaspoon ajwain

2 tomatoes, puréed

1 pound cauliflower, broken into florets

1/2 cup water

1/2 cup almond yogurt

DIRECTIONS

- Press the "Sauté" button to heat up your Instant Pot. Now, heat the oil and sauté the scallions for 1 minute.
- Add garlic and continue to cook an additional 30 seconds or until aromatic.
- Add the garam masala, curry powder, chili pepper, cumin, salt, black pepper, coriander, ajwain, tomatoes, cauliflower, and water.
- Secure the lid. Choose "Manual" mode and High pressure; cook for 3 minutes. Once cooking is complete, use a quick pressure release; carefully remove the lid.
- Pour in the almond yogurt, stir well and serve warm. Bon appétit!

Per serving: 101 Calories; 7.2g Fat; 8.6g Carbs; 2.3g Protein; 3.6g Sugars

49. Dad's Creamy Spinach

(Ready in about 10 minutes | Servings 4)

INGREDIENTS

1 tablespoon olive oil

A bunch of scallions, chopped

3 cloves garlic, smashed

2 pounds spinach, washed

1 cup vegetable broth

1 tablespoon champagne vinegar

Seasoned salt and ground black pepper, to taste

1/4 teaspoon cayenne pepper

1/2 teaspoon dried dill weed

1/2 cup almonds, soaked overnight

2 tablespoons water

2 teaspoons lemon juice

1 tablespoon extra-virgin olive oil

1 teaspoon garlic powder

1 teaspoon onion powder

2 tablespoons green olives, pitted and halved

DIRECTIONS

- Press the "Sauté" button to heat up your Instant Pot. Now, heat the oil and sauté the scallions and garlic for 1 to 2 minutes.
- Add spinach, broth, vinegar, salt, black pepper, cayenne pepper, and dill.
- Secure the lid. Choose "Manual" mode and High pressure; cook for 1 minute. Once cooking is complete, use a quick pressure release; carefully remove the lid.
- Then, drain the almonds and blend them with water, lemon juice, extra-virgin olive oil, garlic powder, onion powder, and olives; mix until well combined.
- Stir the almond cheese into the spinach mixture, and serve. Bon appétit!

Per serving: 108 Calories; 6.2g Fat; 8.6g Carbs; 7.8g Protein; 1.2g Sugars

50. Sticky and Smoky Brown Mushrooms

(Ready in about 10 minutes | Servings 4)

INGREDIENTS

1 pound brown mushrooms

Barbecue sauce:

10 ounces tomato paste

1 cup water

Sea salt and ground black pepper, to taste

1/2 teaspoon porcini powder

1 teaspoon shallot powder

1 teaspoon garlic powder

1 teaspoon mustard seeds

1/2 teaspoon fennel seeds

2 tablespoons lime juice

1 tablespoon coconut aminos

A few drops liquid Stevia

1 teaspoon liquid smoke

DIRECTIONS

- Clean and slice the mushrooms; set them aside.
- Add the remaining ingredients to your Instant Pot and stir to combine; stir in the mushrooms.
- Secure the lid. Choose "Manual" mode and High pressure; cook for 4 minutes. Once cooking is complete, use a natural pressure release; carefully remove the lid. Serve warm.

Per serving: 60 Calories; 0.7g Fat; 8.7g Carbs; 4.6g Protein; 3g Sugars

SNACKS & APPETIZERS

51. Classic Hummus with Tahini

(Ready in about 35 minutes | Servings 8)

INGREDIENTS

10 cups water

3/4 pound dried chickpeas, soaked

2 tablespoons tahini

1/2 lemon, juiced

1 teaspoon granulated garlic

Salt and black pepper, to taste

1/3 teaspoon ground cumin

1/2 teaspoon cayenne pepper

1/2 teaspoon dried basil

3 tablespoon olive oil

DIRECTIONS

- Add water and chickpeas to the Instant Pot. Secure the lid.
- Choose the "Manual" mode and cook for 25 minutes under High pressure. Once cooking is complete, use a natural release; carefully remove the lid.
- Now, drain your chickpeas, reserving the liquid. Transfer the chickpeas to a food processor. Add tahini, lemon juice, and seasonings.
- Puree until it is creamy; gradually pour in the reserved liquid and olive oil until the mixture is smooth and uniform. Serve with a few sprinkles of cayenne pepper. Bon appétit!

Per serving: 186 Calories; 7.7g Fat; 22.8g Carbs; 7.6g Protein; 4g Sugars

52. Pea Dip with Parsley and Mint

(Ready in about 15 minutes | Servings 8)

INGREDIENTS

1 pound dried split peas, rinsed
6 cups vegetable stock
1 tablespoon fresh lemon juice
4 tablespoons extra-virgin olive oil
1 teaspoon fresh mint, chopped

1 tablespoon fresh parsley, chopped
1/2 teaspoon paprika
Sea salt and freshly ground black pepper, to taste

DIRECTIONS

- Add the split peas and vegetable stock to your Instant Pot.
- Secure the lid. Choose the "Manual" mode and cook for 5 minutes under High pressure. Once cooking is complete, use a natural release; carefully remove the lid.
- Transfer the split peas to your food processor; add the remaining ingredients. Process until everything is creamy and well combined. Serve well chilled. Bon appétit!

Per serving: 79 Calories; 4.5g Fat; 4.4g Carbs; 5.6g Protein; 2.3g Sugars

53. Canapés with Sage and Beans

(Ready in about 35 minutes | Servings 6)

INGREDIENTS

2 cups Great Northern beans

1 red onion, peeled and chopped

1 cup water

2 cups vegetable broth

1/2 cup ketchup

Garlic salt, to taste

1 teaspoon chili powder

1/2 teaspoon mixed peppercorns, crushed

1/4 cup dark brown sugar

2 cloves garlic, minced

2 sprigs fresh sage, roughly chopped

2 tablespoons canola oil

6 slices sourdough bread, cut into bite-sized pieces, toasted

DIRECTIONS

- Add the beans, onion, water, and broth to the Instant Pot.
- Secure the lid. Choose the "Soup" mode and High pressure; cook for 25 minutes. Once cooking is complete, use a natural pressure release; carefully remove the lid.
- Add ketchup, salt, chili powder, mixed peppercorns, sugar, garlic, sage, and oil. Press the "Sauté" button.
- Let it simmer an additional 5 to 7 minutes or until everything is heated through. Spoon the hot beans over toast and serve immediately.

Per serving: 393 Calories; 6.5g Fat; 67.4g Carbs; 18.4g Protein; 16.8g Sugars

54. 10-Minute Magic Green Dip

(Ready in about 10 minutes | Servings 10)

INGREDIENTS

1 pound broccoli, broken into florets
1 cup vegetable stock
1/2 cup white onions, chopped
2 garlic cloves, chopped
4 ounces almond milk
1 teaspoon fennel seeds
1 teaspoon mustard seeds
1 tablespoon fresh lime juice

Sea salt and freshly ground black pepper, to taste
4 tablespoons olive oil
1 pound fresh spinach
10 ounces canned artichokes, drained and chopped
1/4 cup vegan mayonnaise

DIRECTIONS

- Add all ingredients, except for the vegan mayonnaise, to your Instant Pot.
- Secure the lid. Choose "Manual" mode and High pressure; cook for 3 minutes. Once cooking is complete, use a quick pressure release; carefully remove the lid.
- Add the vegan mayonnaise, stir and serve warm. Bon appétit!

Per serving: 176 Calories; 13.7g Fat; 9g Carbs; 7g Protein; 1.5g Sugars

55. Spicy Smoked Carrot Dip

(Ready in about 10 minutes | Servings 8)

INGREDIENTS

1 pound carrots, trimmed, peeled, and
   chopped
1/4 cup sesame oil
1/2 teaspoon ground cumin
2 garlic cloves, crushed
1/4 teaspoon dried dill weed

1/2 teaspoon dried basil
1 teaspoon smoked Spanish paprika
Salt and ground white pepper, to your
   liking
1 tablespoon apple cider vinegar

DIRECTIONS

- Add all ingredients to your Instant Pot.
- Secure the lid. Choose "Manual" mode and High pressure; cook for 1 minute. Once cooking is complete, use a quick pressure release; carefully remove the lid.
- Transfer to a serving bowl and serve. Bon appétit!

Per serving: 89 Calories; 7.1g Fat; 6.4g Carbs; 0.7g Protein; 3.1g Sugars

56. Colourful Veggie Sticks

(Ready in about 10 minutes | Servings 5)

INGREDIENTS

1/2 head of broccoli, broken into florets

1/2 head of cauliflower, broken into florets

1 red bell pepper, seeded and diced

1 green bell pepper, seeded and diced

1 orange bell pepper, seeded and diced

9 ounces button mushrooms

2 cups cherry tomatoes

1 teaspoon ground coriander

1 teaspoon cayenne pepper

Coarse sea salt and ground black pepper, to taste

1/4 cup olive oil

DIRECTIONS

- Prepare your Instant Pot by adding 1 cup of water and a metal rack to its bottom.
- Thread your broccoli, cauliflower, bell peppers, mushrooms, and cherry tomatoes onto small bamboo skewers.
- Sprinkle them with coriander, cayenne pepper, salt and black pepper. Drizzle with olive oil and transfer the skewers to the rack.
- Secure the lid. Choose "Manual" mode and High pressure; cook for 3 minutes. Once cooking is complete, use a quick pressure release; carefully remove the lid. Bon appétit!

Per serving: 126 Calories; 9.5g Fat; 9.1g Carbs; 3.7g Protein; 4.4g Sugars

57. Cauliflower and Kalamata Balls

(Ready in about 15 minutes | Servings 8)

INGREDIENTS

1 pound cauliflower, broken into
   florets
2 teaspoons vegan margarine
1/3 cup coconut cream
Sea salt, to taste

1/3 teaspoon ground black pepper
A pinch of freshly grated nutmeg
2 cloves garlic, peeled
3 tablespoons Kalamata olives, pitted
2 tablespoons smoked paprika

DIRECTIONS

- Add 1 cup of water and a steamer basket to the bottom of your Instant Pot.
- Then, arrange the cauliflower and kohlrabi in the steamer basket.
- Secure the lid. Choose "Manual" mode and High pressure; cook for 2 minutes. Once cooking is complete, use a quick pressure release; carefully remove the lid.
- Purée your cauliflower along with the remaining ingredients in a food processor.
- Form the mixture into balls and roll each ball into smoked paprika powder. Arrange on a nice serving platter. Bon appétit!

Per serving: 60 Calories; 4.8g Fat; 4g Carbs; 1.5g Protein; 1.1g Sugars

58. Spicy Chard and Carrot Dip

(Ready in about 15 minutes | Servings 4)

INGREDIENTS

2 cups carrots, peeled and chopped

10 ounces fresh or frozen (and thawed) chard, torn into pieces

Sea salt, to taste

1/4 teaspoon ground black pepper, to taste

1/2 teaspoon garlic powder

1/2 teaspoon shallot power

1/2 teaspoon fennel seeds

1 teaspoon cayenne pepper

1 teaspoon Sriracha chili sauce

2 tablespoons coconut oil

3/4 cup vegetable broth

1/3 cup coconut cream

DIRECTIONS

- Add all ingredients, except for the coconut cream, to your Instant Pot.
- Secure the lid. Choose "Manual" mode and High pressure; cook for 2 minutes. Once cooking is complete, use a quick pressure release; carefully remove the lid.
- Transfer the vegetable mixture to your food processor; add the coconut cream and purée the mixture until uniform, creamy, and smooth. Serve warm. Bon appétit!

Per serving: 140 Calories; 11.3g Fat; 9.1g Carbs; 2.3g Protein; 4.4g Sugars

59. Cauliflower Bites with Vegan Parmesan

(Ready in about 10 minutes | Servings 4)

INGREDIENTS

1 pound cauliflower, broken into
  florets
Kosher salt and freshly ground black
  pepper, to taste
2 garlic cloves, chopped
1 teaspoon rosemary
1 teaspoon dried basil

2 tablespoons sesame oil
Vegan Parmesan:
1/2 cup sesame seeds
1/2 teaspoon sea salt
1/2 teaspoon oregano
1/4 teaspoon cumin seeds
1/4 teaspoon ground fennel seeds

DIRECTIONS

- Add 1 cup of water and a steamer basket to your Instant Pot.
- Now, arrange the cauliflower florets on the steamer basket. Add salt, black pepper, garlic, rosemary, basil, and sesame oil.
- Secure the lid. Choose "Manual" mode and Low pressure; cook for 3 minutes. Once cooking is complete, use a quick pressure release; carefully remove the lid.
- Thoroughly combine the remaining ingredients in your food processor until the mixture has the texture of Parmigiano-Reggiano granular cheese.
- Top your cauliflower with Vegan Parmesan and serve immediately. Bon appétit!

Per serving: 209 Calories; 18.6g Fat; 8.3g Carbs; 6.1g Protein; 2.3g Sugars

60. Saucy Mushroom Bites

(Ready in about 10 minutes | Servings 4)

INGREDIENTS

1/4 cup port wine

1/4 cup coconut milk

1 tablespoon tamari sauce

2 tablespoons sesame oil

1 teaspoon ginger-garlic paste

1 ½ pounds button mushrooms

Sea salt and ground pepper, to taste

1 teaspoon red pepper flakes

2 tablespoons fresh chives, roughly
chopped

DIRECTIONS

- Add wine, coconut milk, tamari sauce, sesame oil, ginger-garlic paste and mushrooms to a ceramic bowl; cover and let it marinate in your refrigerator for 40 minutes.
- Add the mushrooms along with their marinade to the Instant Pot. Add salt, black pepper, and red pepper flakes.
- Secure the lid. Choose "Manual" mode and High pressure; cook for 5 minutes. Once cooking is complete, use a quick pressure release; carefully remove the lid.
- Serve with toothpicks garnished with fresh chives. Enjoy!

Per serving: 110 Calories; 7.9g Fat; 6.8g Carbs; 5.9g Protein; 4.5g Sugars

61. Khumban da Appetizer

(Ready in about 10 minutes | Servings 6)

INGREDIENTS

2 tablespoons olive oil

30 ounces king oyster mushrooms, brushed clean and sliced

2 cloves garlic, minced

1 teaspoon dried rosemary

1 teaspoon dried basil

1/2 teaspoon dried thyme

1 bay leaf

1/2 cup vegetable broth

1/4 teaspoon freshly ground black pepper

1/4 teaspoon cayenne pepper

Kosher salt, to taste

1/2 cup tomato sauce

1 ripe tomato, puréed

2 tablespoons fresh watercress leaves, chopped

DIRECTIONS

- Add all ingredients, except for the watercress leaves, to your Instant Pot.
- Secure the lid. Choose "Manual" mode and High pressure; cook for 5 minutes. Once cooking is complete, use a quick pressure release; carefully remove the lid.
- Ladle into individual bowls, garnish with watercress leaves and serve warm. Bon appétit!

Per serving: 105 Calories; 5.7g Fat; 9g Carbs; 0.9g Protein; 2.7g Sugars

62. Braised Kale with Red Wine

(Ready in about 10 minutes | Servings 4)

INGREDIENTS

1 pound Collards, torn into pieces

1 ½ tablespoons sesame oil

1 teaspoon ginger-garlic paste

Sea salt and ground black pepper, to
taste

1/2 teaspoon mustard seeds

1/2 teaspoon fennel seeds

3/4 cup water

1/4 cup dry red wine

DIRECTIONS

- Simply throw all of the above ingredients into your Instant Pot.
- Secure the lid. Choose "Manual" mode and High pressure; cook for 2 minutes. Once cooking is complete, use a quick pressure release; carefully remove the lid.
- Ladle into individual bowls and serve warm. Bon appétit!

Per serving: 91 Calories; 5.9g Fat; 7.5g Carbs; 3.7g Protein; 1.1g Sugars

KETOGENIC RECIPES

63. Tofu in African Spicy Sauce

(Ready in about 1 hour 10 minutes | Servings 4)

INGREDIENTS

1 (15-ounce) block firm tofu, pressed, drained, and cubed

1/2 cup vegetable stock

1 tablespoon dark vinegar

Himalayan salt, to taste

1/4 teaspoon ground black pepper, or more to taste

1/2 teaspoon cayenne pepper

2 tablespoons coconut oil, melted

2 garlic cloves, crushed

1/2 teaspoon ground cumin

1/2 teaspoon dried marjoram

2 fresh African bird's eye chili peppers, seeded and finely chopped

1/2 cup scallions, chopped

DIRECTIONS

- Purée all ingredients, except for the tofu and vegetable stock, in a food processor until creamy and uniform.
- Transfer this mixture to a ceramic container; add tofu, cover your container and place in the refrigerator for 1 hour.
- Transfer the mixture to your Instant Pot. Pour in vegetable stock and stir to combine.
- Secure the lid. Choose "Manual" mode and High pressure; cook for 2 minutes. Once cooking is complete, use a quick pressure release; carefully remove the lid.

Per serving: 185 Calories; 13.8g Fat; 4.2g Carbs; 12.7g Protein; 2.1g Sugars

64. Traditional Broccoli Rabe Soup

(Ready in about 10 minutes | Servings 4)

INGREDIENTS

2 tablespoons grapeseed oil

1 white onion, thinly sliced

2 garlic cloves, minced

1 bird chili, minced

1 (1-inch) piece fresh ginger root, peeled and grated

1 pound broccoli rabe, cut into pieces

4 cups warm water

2 tablespoons vegetable bouillon granules

1 celery, trimmed and diced

1 carrot, trimmed and sliced

3/4 cup acorn squash, peeled and cubed

1/4 cup dry white wine

Celery salt and ground black pepper, to taste

DIRECTIONS

- Press the "Sauté" button to heat up your Instant Pot. Heat the oil and sauté the onions, stirring frequently, until caramelized.
- Add the remaining ingredients and gently stir to combine.
- Secure the lid. Choose "Manual" mode and Low pressure; cook for 5 minutes. Once cooking is complete, use a quick pressure release; carefully remove the lid.
- Lastly, purée the soup with an immersion blender until smooth and uniform; then, return the soup to the Instant Pot. Ladle into soup bowls and serve hot. Bon appétit!

Per serving: 121 Calories; 7.6g Fat; 5.5g Carbs; 4.3g Protein; 1.1g Sugars

65. Celery Soup with Thai Peppercorns

(Ready in about 10 minutes | Servings 4)

INGREDIENTS

2 tablespoons olive oil

1/2 cup leeks, chopped

3 cups celery with leaves, chopped

2 cloves garlic, smashed

1 (2-inch) piece young galangal,
   peeled and chopped

1 teaspoon shallot powder

2 fresh bird chilies, seeded and finely
   chopped

4 cups water

2 tablespoons vegetable bouillon
   granules

1/2 teaspoon Thai white peppercorns,
   ground

Sea salt, to taste

1 bay leaf

1/4 cup coconut cream, unsweetened

2 sprigs cilantro, coarsely chopped

DIRECTIONS

- Press the "Sauté" button to heat up your Instant Pot. Heat the oil and sauté the leeks until tender or about 2 minutes.
- Add the celery, garlic, and galangal; continue to cook an additional 2 minutes.
- Next, add the shallot powder, bird chilies, water, vegetable bouillon granules, Thai white peppercorns, salt, and bay leaf.
- Secure the lid. Choose "Manual" mode and High pressure; cook for 2 minutes. Once cooking is complete, use a quick pressure release; carefully remove the lid.
- Afterwards, purée the soup with an immersion blender until smooth and uniform; then, return the soup to the Instant Pot.
- Add the coconut cream and press the "Sauté" button again. Let it simmer until everything is heated through.
- Ladle into soup bowls, garnish with cilantro, and serve hot. Enjoy!

Per serving: 141 Calories; 11.1g Fat; 9.1g Carbs; 2.2g Protein; 4.2g Sugars

66. Creamed Cauliflower Soup with Paprika

(Ready in about 15 minutes | Servings 4)

INGREDIENTS

3 teaspoons sesame oil

1 shallot, chopped

2 cloves garlic, minced

1 celery stalk, chopped

3/4 pound cauliflower, broken into
   florets

4 cups water

4 vegan bouillon cubes

1 teaspoon fresh coriander, chopped

1/2 teaspoon ground cumin

1 teaspoon paprika

Himalayan salt and freshly ground
   black pepper, to taste

1/2 cup almond milk, unsweetened

2 tablespoons fresh parsley, chopped

DIRECTIONS

- Press the "Sauté" button to heat up your Instant Pot. Heat the oil and sauté the shallot until tender or about 2 minutes.
- Add garlic and continue to cook for 30 seconds more, stirring frequently.
- Add the celery, cauliflower, water, bouillon cubes, fresh coriander, cumin, paprika, salt, and black pepper.
- Secure the lid. Choose "Manual" mode and Low pressure; cook for 3 minutes. Once cooking is complete, use a quick pressure release; carefully remove the lid.
- Then, add almond milk, press the "Sauté" button again and let it simmer an additional 4 minutes or until everything is heated through.
- Afterwards, purée the soup with an immersion blender until smooth and uniform; then, return the soup to the Instant Pot.
- Ladle into soup bowls, garnish with fresh parsley, and serve warm. Bon appétit!

Per serving: 144 Calories; 11.4g Fat; 9.2g Carbs; 3.3g Protein; 3.5g Sugars

67. Ketogenic Naan with Peppers

(Ready in about 20 minutes | Servings 6)

INGREDIENTS

3 teaspoons canola oil

1/3 teaspoon cumin seeds

2 red bell pepper, seeded and sliced

1 green bell pepper, seeded and sliced

1 garlic clove, minced

1 teaspoon dhania

1 teaspoon chili powder

1/2 teaspoon haldi

Sea salt and ground black pepper, to taste

1 tablespoon fresh lemon juice

Coconut Flour Naan:

1/2 cup coconut flour

1/2 teaspoon baking powder

1 ½ tablespoons ground psyllium husk
  powder

1/2 teaspoon salt

1/4 cup coconut oil, melted

1 ½ cups boiling water

1 tablespoon coconut oil, for frying

DIRECTIONS

- Press the "Sauté" button to heat up your Instant Pot. Heat the canola oil until sizzling. Once hot, sauté the cumin seeds for 40 seconds.
- Now, add the peppers, garlic, and spices.
- Secure the lid. Choose "Manual" mode and Low pressure; cook for 4 minutes.
- Once cooking is complete, use a quick pressure release; carefully remove the lid. Add lemon juice.
- To make the naan, in a mixing bowl, combine coconut flour with baking powder, psyllium and salt; mix to combine well.
- Add 1/4 cup of coconut oil; add the hot water to form a dough; let it rest for 10 minutes at room temperature.
- Now, divide the dough into 6 balls; flatten the balls on a working surface.
- Heat up a pan with 1 tablespoon of coconut oil over a medium-high flame. Fry the naan breads until they are golden.
- Serve these naans with Indian peppers and enjoy!

Per serving: 348 Calories; 38.7g Fat; 3.2g Carbs; 0.6g Protein; 1.7g Sugars

68. Indian Mushroom Curry with Tofu

(Ready in about 10 minutes | Servings 4)

INGREDIENTS

1 tablespoon coconut oil

1 ½ cups button mushrooms, sliced

1 garlic clove, minced

8 ounces firm tofu, pressed and cubed

8 ounces coconut milk

2 tablespoons curry paste

1 tablespoon Garam Masala

Sea salt and ground black pepper, to taste

2 tablespoons tomato paste

1 shallot, chopped

1 cup vegetable stock

2 heaping tablespoons coriander, chopped

DIRECTIONS

- Press the "Sauté" button to heat up your Instant Pot. Heat the oil and sauté the mushrooms and garlic about 2 minutes or until fragrant.
- Add the cubed tofu to your Instant Pot.
- In a food processor, blend the milk, curry, Garam Masala, salt, pepper, tomato paste, and shallot. Add this mixture to the Instant Pot.
- Pour in the vegetable broth and secure the lid.
- Choose "Manual" mode and High pressure; cook for 5 minutes. Once cooking is complete, use a quick pressure release; carefully remove the lid.
- Afterwards, press the "Sauté" button one more time and let it simmer until the sauce has reduced. Serve warm.

Per serving: 157 Calories; 9.5g Fat; 9.3g Carbs; 12.4g Protein; 3.2g Sugars

69. Easy Green Beans with Mushrooms

(Ready in about 10 minutes | Servings 4)

INGREDIENTS

2 tablespoons olive oil

1/2 cup scallions, chopped

2 cloves garlic, minced

1 cup white mushrooms, chopped

3/4 pound green beans

1 cup vegetable broth

Sea salt and ground black pepper, to taste

1 teaspoon red pepper flakes, crushed

DIRECTIONS

- Press the "Sauté" button to heat up your Instant Pot. Heat the oil and sauté scallions until softened or about 2 minutes.
- Then, add garlic and mushrooms; continue to cook an additional minute or so.
- Add the other ingredients; gently stir to combine.
- Secure the lid. Choose "Manual" mode and Low pressure; cook for 3 minutes. Once cooking is complete, use a quick pressure release; carefully remove the lid.
- Serve warm and enjoy!

Per serving: 106 Calories; 7.7g Fat; 7g Carbs; 3.5g Protein; 1.7g Sugars

70. Easiest Pepperonata Ever

(Ready in about 15 minutes | Servings 4)

INGREDIENTS

2 tablespoons grapeseed oil

1/2 cup onions, chopped

2 green bell peppers, seeded and
chopped

1 red bell pepper, seeded and chopped

1 yellow bell pepper, seeded and
chopped

1 red chili pepper, seeded and minced

2 tomatoes, pureed

2 garlic cloves, crushed

1 tablespoon balsamic vinegar

1 teaspoon dried basil

1 teaspoon dried oregano

1 teaspoon dried thyme

1/4 cup Italian dry white wine

3/4 cup vegetable broth

Sea salt and ground black pepper, to
taste

1 teaspoon paprika

2 tablespoons fresh Italian parsley,
roughly chopped

DIRECTIONS

- Press the "Sauté" button to heat up your Instant Pot. Heat the oil and sauté the onion until it is softened.
- Add the other ingredients, except for the Italian parsley.
- Secure the lid. Choose "Manual" mode and High pressure; cook for 3 minutes. Once cooking is complete, use a quick pressure release; carefully remove the lid.
- Press the "Sauté" button again to thicken the cooking liquid; let it simmer for 3 to 4 minutes.
- Divide between four serving bowls and garnish with fresh parsley. Bon appétit!

Per serving: 308 Calories; 30.6g Fat; 7.9g Carbs; 5.6g Protein; 1.1g Sugars

71. Croatian-Style Greens with Dry Sherry

(Ready in about 5 minutes | Servings 4)

INGREDIENTS

2 tablespoons olive oil

1 teaspoon garlic, minced

1 cup scallions, chopped

1 ripe tomato, puréed

1 pound Swiss chard, torn into pieces

1/4 cup dry sherry

2 tablespoons dried parsley

1/4 teaspoon basil

DIRECTIONS

- Press the "Sauté" button to heat up your Instant Pot. Heat the oil and sauté garlic approximately 40 seconds or until aromatic.
- Add the remaining ingredients and stir to combine well.
- Secure the lid. Choose "Manual" mode and Low pressure; cook for 2 minutes. Once cooking is complete, use a quick pressure release; carefully remove the lid.
- Serve in individual bowls and enjoy!

Per serving: 109 Calories; 7.1g Fat; 8g Carbs; 2.8g Protein; 2.8g Sugars

72. Cabbage with Tempeh and Cilantro

(Ready in about 10 minutes | Servings 3)

INGREDIENTS

2 tablespoons sesame oil

1/2 cup scallions, chopped

2 cups cabbages, shredded

6 ounces tempeh, cubed

1 tablespoon coconut aminos

1 cup vegetable stock

2 garlic cloves, minced

1 tablespoon lemon juice

Salt and pepper, to taste

1/4 teaspoon paprika

1/4 cup fresh cilantro, roughly
chopped

DIRECTIONS

- Press the "Sauté" button to heat up your Instant Pot. Heat the sesame oil and sauté the scallions until tender and fragrant.
- Then, add the cabbage, tempeh, coconut aminos, vegetable stock, garlic, lemon juice, salt, pepper, and paprika.
- Secure the lid. Choose "Manual" mode and Low pressure; cook for 3 minutes. Once cooking is complete, use a quick pressure release; carefully remove the lid.
- Press the "Sauté" button to thicken the sauce if desired. Divide between serving bowls, garnish with fresh cilantro, and serve warm. Bon appétit!

Per serving: 172 Calories; 11.9g Fat; 8.9g Carbs; 10.1g Protein; 2.1g Sugars

73. Pumpkin and Leek Chowder

(Ready in about 15 minutes | Servings 4)

INGREDIENTS

10 ounces coconut milk

10 ounces vegetable stock

1 garlic cloves, minced

1 teaspoon fresh ginger root, grated

4 tablespoons almond butter

Sea salt and ground black pepper, to
  taste

1/2 teaspoon turmeric powder

A pinch of grated nutmeg

1/2 teaspoon ground coriander

10 ounces pumpkin, cubed

1/3 cup leek, white part only, finely
  sliced

DIRECTIONS

- Place the milk, stock, garlic, ginger, almond butter, salt, black pepper, turmeric powder, nutmeg, coriander, and pumpkin in your Instant Pot.
- Secure the lid. Choose "Manual" mode and High pressure; cook for 10 minutes. Once cooking is complete, use a natural pressure release; carefully remove the lid.
- Now, blend your chowder with a stick blender. Ladle your chowder into serving bowls and top with leeks. Bon appétit!

Per serving: 157 Calories; 12.3g Fat; 9.4g Carbs; 3.4g Protein; 4.7g Sugars

74. Roma Tomato and Mushroom Stew

(Ready in about 20 minutes | Servings 4)

INGREDIENTS

2 tablespoons sesame oil

1 red onion, chopped

1 teaspoon ginger-garlic paste

1 celery stalk, sliced

1 carrot, sliced

3 cups brown mushrooms, sliced

2 ripe Roma tomatoes, puréed

1 cup vegetable broth, preferably
   homemade

1 (12-ounce) bottle amber beer

2 bay leaves

1/2 teaspoon caraway seeds

1/4 teaspoon cumin seeds

1/2 teaspoon fenugreek seeds

Sea salt and ground black pepper, to
   taste

1 teaspoon Hungarian hot paprika

1 tablespoon soy sauce

DIRECTIONS

- Press the "Sauté" button to heat up your Instant Pot. Heat the sesame oil and cook the onions for 2 to 3 minutes or until tender and translucent.
- Now, add the ginger-garlic paste, celery, carrot and mushrooms; continue to cook for a further 2 minutes or until fragrant.
- Add the remaining ingredients, except for the soy sauce.
- Secure the lid. Choose "Manual" mode and High pressure; cook for 10 minutes. Once cooking is complete, use a quick pressure release; carefully remove the lid.
- Ladle into individual bowls, add a few drizzles of soy sauce and serve warm. Bon appétit!

Per serving: 136 Calories; 7.3g Fat; 9.3g Carbs; 2.6g Protein; 3.5g Sugars

75. Thick Tomato Soup with Herbs

(Ready in about 15 minutes | Servings 4)

INGREDIENTS

2 tablespoons olive oil

1 shallot, chopped

1 celery, diced

3 ripe medium-sized tomatoes, puréed

4 cups roasted vegetable stock

1 teaspoon granulated garlic

1/2 teaspoon rosemary

1/2 teaspoon lemon thyme

Himalayan salt and ground white pepper, to taste

1 bay leaf

4-5 whole cloves

1/2 cup almond milk, unsweetened

2 heaping tablespoons fresh parsley, roughly chopped

DIRECTIONS

- Press the "Sauté" button to heat up your Instant Pot. Heat the olive oil and sauté the shallot and celery until softened.
- Now, add the tomatoes, stock, garlic, rosemary, lemon thyme, salt, black pepper, bay leaf, cloves, and milk; stir to combine well.
- Secure the lid. Choose "Manual" mode and High pressure; cook for 8 minutes. Once cooking is complete, use a natural pressure release; carefully remove the lid.
- Ladle into individual bowls and top each serving with fresh parsley. Serve hot and enjoy!

Per serving: 136 Calories; 9.8g Fat; 5.8g Carbs; 7.2g Protein; 4.3g Sugars

33672840R00053

Made in the USA
Middletown, DE
16 January 2019